For all my teachers,
thank you for your guidance and support.

All rights reserved. Published in the United States by Dragonfly Books, an imprint of Random House
Children's Books, a division of Penguin Random House LLC, New York. Originally published in hardcover in
the United States by Crown Books for Young Readers, New York, 2021.

Dragonfly Books and colophon are registered trademarks of Penguin Random House LLC.

Visit us on the Web! rhcbooks.com

Educators and librarians, for a variety of teaching tools, visit us at RHTeachersLibrarians.com

The Library of Congress has cataloged the hardcover edition of this work as follows:
Names: Ignotofsky, Rachel, author.
Title: What's inside a flower? : and other questions about science & nature / by Rachel Ignotofsky
Description: First edition. | New York : Crown Books for Young Readers, [2021] | Audience: Ages 4–7 |
Audience: Grades K–1 | Summary: "In the launch of a new nonfiction picture book series, Rachel Ignotofsky's
distinctive art style and engaging, informative text clearly answers any questions a child (or adult) could have
about flowers"—Provided by publisher.
Identifiers: LCCN 2020010743 | ISBN 978-0-593-17647-4 (hardcover) | ISBN 978-0-593-17651-1 (library binding) |
ISBN 978-0-593-17650-4 (ebook)
Subjects: LCSH: Flowers—Juvenile literature. | Flowers—Morphology—Juvenile literature. | Plant morphology—
Juvenile literature.
Classification: LCC QK653 .I36 2021 | DDC 582.1—dc23

ISBN 978-0-593-17648-1 (pbk.)

MANUFACTURED IN CHINA

10 9 8 7 6 5 4 3 2

First Dragonfly Books Edition 2023

RACHEL IGNOTOFSKY

WHAT'S INSIDE A
FLOWER?

AND OTHER QUESTIONS ABOUT SCIENCE & NATURE

Dragonfly Books —✦— New York

ORCID

HYACINTH

TULIP

POPPY

ROSE

BUTTERCUP

Flowers live everywhere.

LILY

FUCHSIA

DAFFODIL

BLACK-EYED SUSAN

QUEEN ANNE'S LACE

THISTLE

They bloom in . . .

bustling cities,

lush jungles,

soggy swamps,

CATTAIL

WATER LILY

blistering deserts,

BARREL CACTUS

PRICKLY PEAR CACTUS

STARFISH CACTUS

ROCK-JASMINE

EDELWEISS

ALPINE MOON DAISY

and high up on rocky mountaintops.

ALPINE BELLFLOWER

Flowers are found growing on trees . . .

in orchards,

on the vines of fruits,

VEGETABLES WITH SEEDS ARE SCIENTIFICALLY CONSIDERED FRUIT.

WINECUP FLOWER

PURPLE PRAIRIE CLOVER

BLUE SPRING-DAISY

PRAIRIE ONION

PRAYING MANTIS

GRASSHOPPER

in grassy fields,

and in fancy gardens.

HYACINTH

DAFFODIL

LAVENDER

Flowers come in many colors,

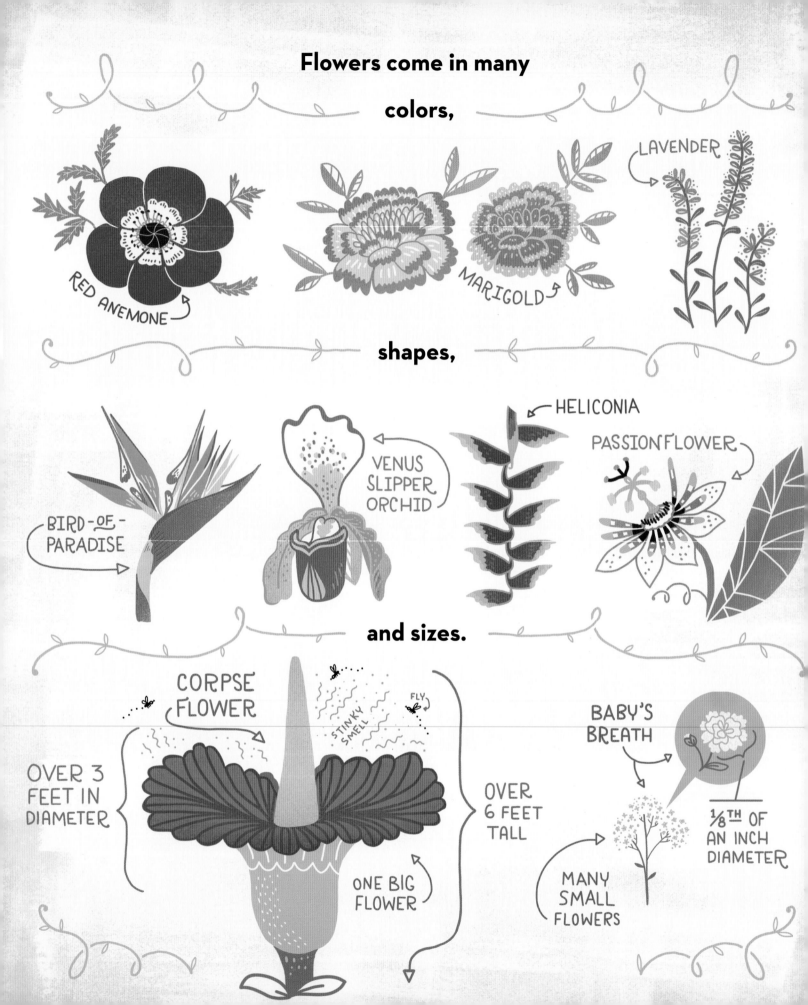

RED ANEMONE

MARIGOLD

LAVENDER

shapes,

BIRD-OF-PARADISE

VENUS SLIPPER ORCHID

HELICONIA

PASSIONFLOWER

and sizes.

CORPSE FLOWER

STINKY SMELL

FLY

OVER 3 FEET IN DIAMETER

OVER 6 FEET TALL

ONE BIG FLOWER

BABY'S BREATH

1/8 TH OF AN INCH DIAMETER

MANY SMALL FLOWERS

But how does a flower grow?

Why do flowers bloom on plants?

What's inside a flower?

**A flower starts as
a seed underground.**

SOIL

① ② SEED ③ ④

**The seed will begin
to grow roots and
its first leaves.**

EARTHWORM

Above ground and below, bugs,
bacteria, and fungi all munch, crunch,
and wiggle their way through dirt.

YUM!

DEAD LEAF

ANT

YUM!

SNAIL

They are called decomposers.
Decomposers eat waste like
garbage, dead things, and poop!

By breaking down
waste, decomposers
make new soil.

FUNGUS

MITE

BACTERIA

Soil is the perfect
place for a seed to
grow into a flower.

NEMATODE

With time the seed will become a much larger plant.

SOW BUG

RAINWATER

MILLIPEDE

SOIL

The flower's roots spread deep into the ground, keeping the plant sturdy so it can grow tall.

WATER

ROOT HAIR

CALCIUM

SULFUR

MAGNESIUM

POTASSIUM

PHOSPHORUS

NITROGEN

MINERALS

Rich soil has water and minerals that a plant needs to grow.

STEM

ANT

Rainwater soaks into the soil, traveling down to the roots.

MAIN ROOT

WATER

The minerals in the soil help the plant grow strong.

The root hairs slurp up the water and minerals.

EARTHWORM

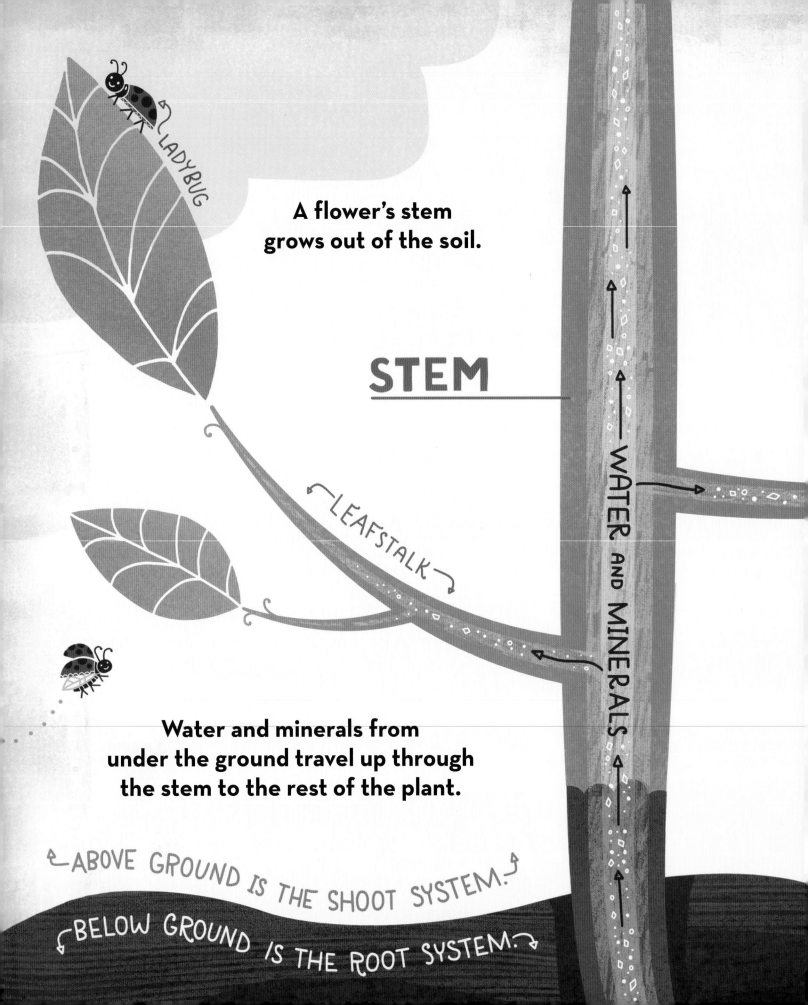

LADYBUG

A flower's stem
grows out of the soil.

STEM

LEAFSTALK

WATER AND MINERALS

Water and minerals from
under the ground travel up through
the stem to the rest of the plant.

ABOVE GROUND IS THE SHOOT SYSTEM.

BELOW GROUND IS THE ROOT SYSTEM.

The stem holds up the plant's leaves and flowers high above the ground.

CRUNCH

MUNCH

CATERPILLAR

LEAF

Leaves are food for many animals.

YUM! A LEAF!

APHID

YUM! AN APHID!

RAWRR!

LOOK! AN APHID IS HAVING A SNACK, WHILE A LADYBUG STALKS ITS TINY PREY.

SOIL

Leaves have the special job of absorbing sunshine.

Plants turn sunlight into food in a process called photosynthesis.

WOW!

LEAF

SUNLIGHT

SUNLIGHT

↱PHOTOSYNTHESIS↲

DURING PHOTOSYNTHESIS, PLANTS USE:
SUNLIGHT AND WATER AND CARBON DIOXIDE FROM THE AIR...

ENERGY

$+$

H_2O

$+$

CO_2

...TO MAKE SUGAR (GLUCOSE), WHICH PLANTS USE AS FOOD!

WHERE PHOTOSYNTHESIS HAPPENS

MICROSCOPIC **PLANT CELL**

Turning sunlight into food is a plant's superpower.

Just like people need food
to grow big and strong,
a flower needs sunshine,
water, and minerals to grow.

When a flowering plant gets big enough, buds will appear.

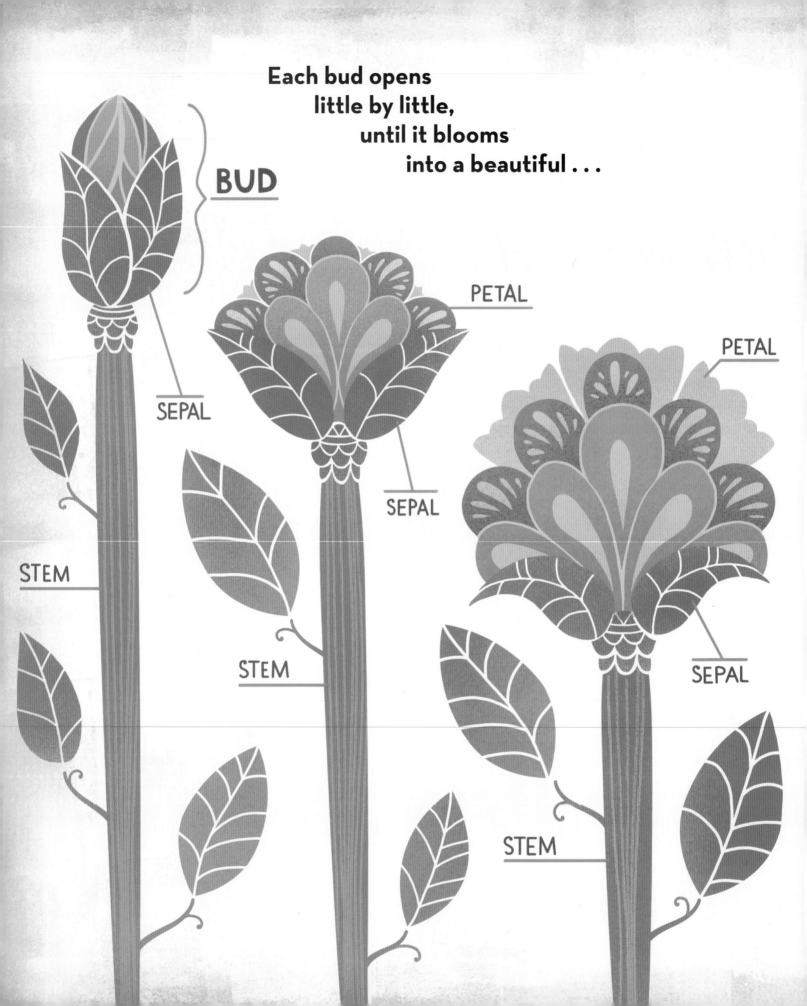

Each bud opens little by little, until it blooms into a beautiful . . .

BUD

PETAL

PETAL

SEPAL

SEPAL

SEPAL

STEM

STEM

STEM

FLOWER!

PETALS

SEPAL

STEM

LEAF

Look inside a flower to see where seeds are made.

PISTIL
STIGMA
STYLE
OVULE
OVARY

POLLEN

STAMEN
ANTHER
FILAMENT

PETALS

SEPAL

STEM

LEAF

The stamen make fluffy grains called pollen.

POLLEN

STAMEN

ANTHER

FILAMENT

The pistil has a sticky stigma and tiny egg cells called ovules.

STIGMA

STYLE

PISTIL

OVARY

OVULE

A new seed can only grow when pollen land on a flower's stigma.

POLLEN

This is called pollination.

POLLINATION IS BETWEEN FLOWERS THAT ARE THE SAME TYPE (SPECIES).

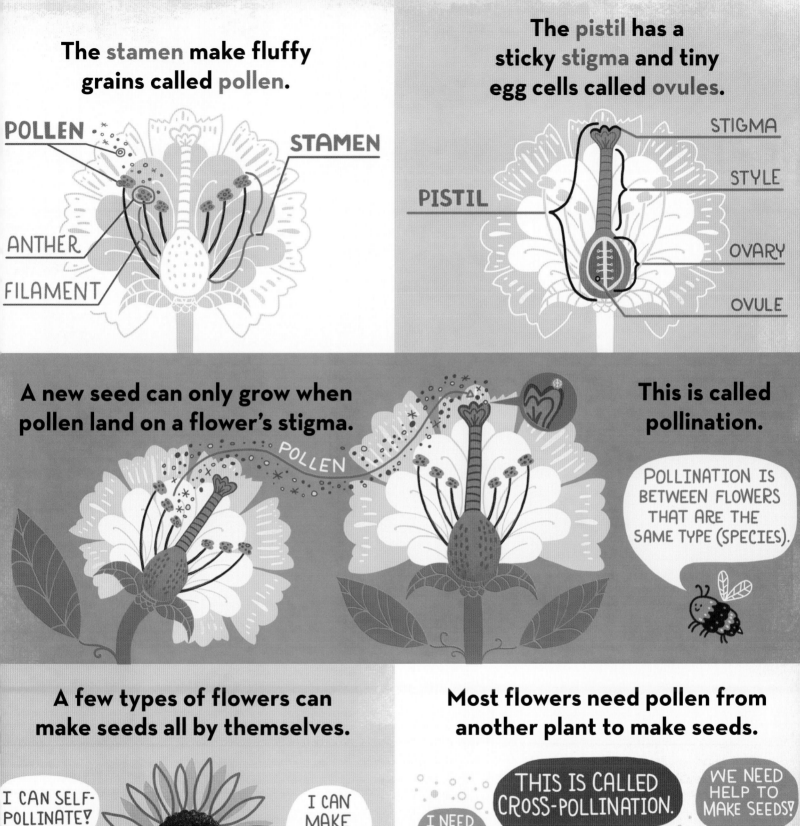

A few types of flowers can make seeds all by themselves.

I CAN SELF-POLLINATE!

I CAN MAKE SEEDS ON MY OWN.

SUNFLOWER

Most flowers need pollen from another plant to make seeds.

I NEED YOUR POLLEN!

THIS IS CALLED CROSS-POLLINATION.

WE NEED HELP TO MAKE SEEDS!

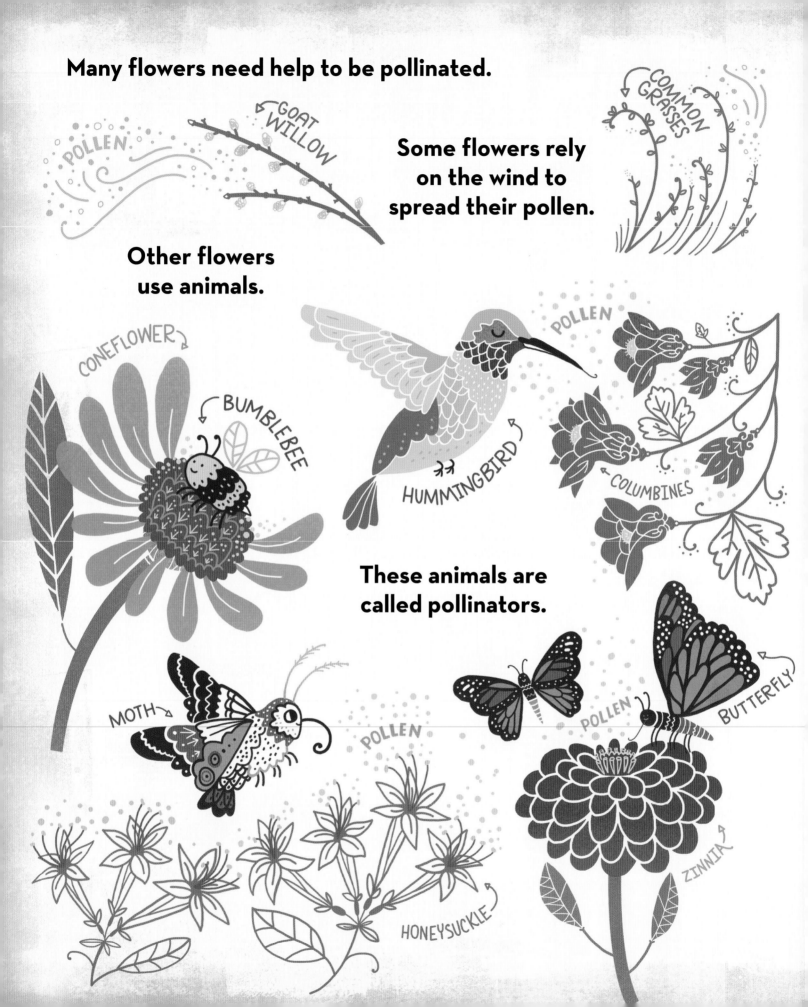

Many flowers need help to be pollinated.

POLLEN

GOAT WILLOW

Some flowers rely on the wind to spread their pollen.

COMMON GRASSES

Other flowers use animals.

CONEFLOWER

BUMBLEBEE

POLLEN

HUMMINGBIRD

COLUMBINES

These animals are called pollinators.

MOTH

POLLEN

POLLEN

BUTTERFLY

ZINNIA

HONEYSUCKLE

Flowers create nectar that many pollinators love to eat.

POLLINATOR

NECTAR

YUM

POLLEN

STAMEN

POLLEN

CAVE NECTAR BAT →

Bees, butterflies, birds, and bats all reach inside the flowers for a tasty treat.

POLLEN

The pollen sticks to their bodies . . .

and as the pollinators snack from flower to flower . . .

YUM! NECTAR!

POLLEN

NECTAR

POLLEN

. . . they spread pollen and help to create seeds!

Flowers attract pollinators in different ways.

POLLEN

PANSY

POLLEN

AZALEA

Many flowers have colorful petals. They are like neon signs saying "Nectar's here!"

MOONFLOWER

PERUVIAN APPLE CACTUS

Some flowers have strong smells to attract pollinators.

Night-blooming flowers smell especially sweet so pollinators can find them in the dark.

A flower petal's shape makes feeding easy for local pollinators.

POLLEN

MARIGOLD

DAISIES

Some petals are shaped like a landing pad for bugs . . .

TRUMPET CREEPER

POLLEN

while other flowers are perfect for long tongues and beaks.

BUTTERCUP

POLLEN

The more pollinators that visit a flower, the more chances there are for seeds to be made.

Many plants use seeds to reproduce and spread new plants around the world!

Flowers create new seeds through pollination.

Pollen lands on a flower's stigma and grows a tiny tube to travel down into an ovule (an egg cell).

POLLEN

STIGMA

TUBE

MALE GAMETES

POLLEN

STIGMA

THIS IS HOW POLLEN BEGINS TO FERTILIZE AN OVULE.

STYLE

OVARY

TUBE

OVULE

A GRAIN OF POLLEN AND AN OVULE EACH HAVE HALF OF WHAT'S NEEDED TO MAKE A SEED.

When the pollen grain and ovule join, a brand-new seed begins to grow.

As the seeds get bigger, the flower begins to change.

Petals wilt and fall . . .

as a fruit or pod grows to protect the precious seed.

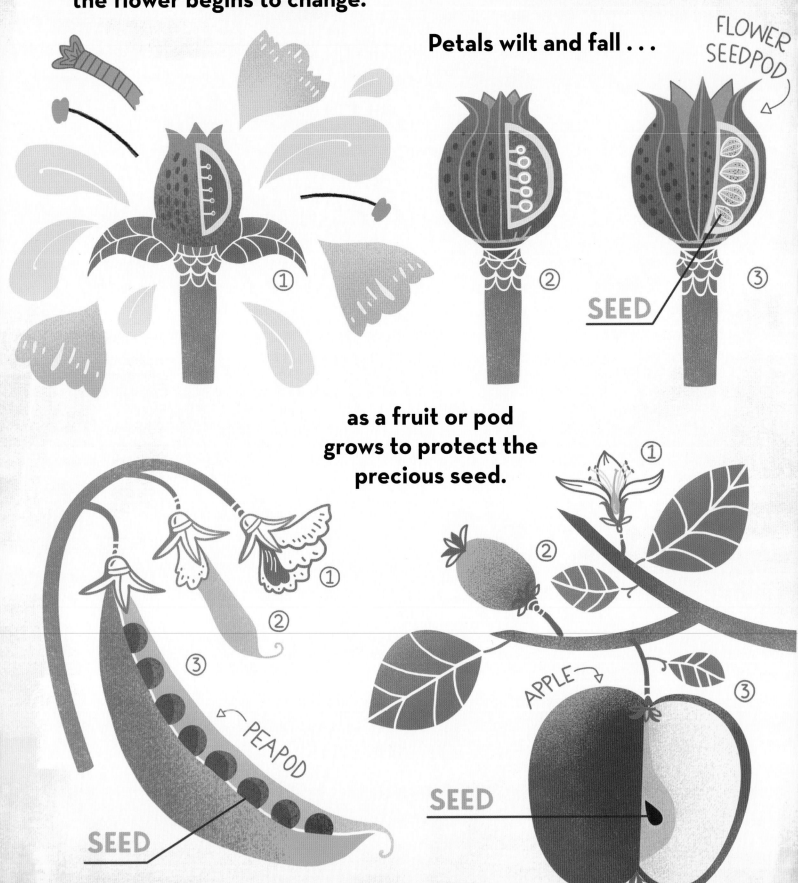

FLOWER
SEEDPOD

① ② ③

SEED

① ② ③

PEAPOD

SEED

① ② ③

APPLE

SEED

GOLDEN RAIN
TREE SEEDPOD

CHICKPEA

ROYAL POINCIANA SEEDPOD

BOTTLE TREE
SEEDPOD

CHERRY

AVOCADO

CHESTNUT

POPPY
POD

MAPLE SEED

SWEET GUM
SEEDPODS

CHILI PEPPER

LOTUS POD

The fruits, husks, and pods that protect seeds come in all different shapes and sizes.

STAR ANISE

PEONY
SEEDPOD

CUCUMBER

POMEGRANATE

ORANGE

ACORN

TEXAS MOUNTAIN
LAUREL POD

COMMON
BEECH NUT

WITCH
HAZEL

Time passes and seeds become ready to be planted.

Some seeds will burst out of their pods and grow wherever they fall.

Other seeds will be eaten by animals and scattered when they poop.

Seeds travel near and far.

They roll down hills, fly on the wind, and float away in water.

Some seeds have "wings" to help them glide.

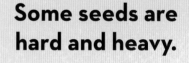

Some seeds are hard and heavy.

There are even seeds with hooks to catch a ride on a passerby.

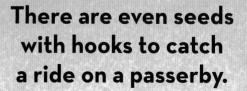

Once a seed finds a spot in the soil,
a new plant will grow.

And a new flower will bloom.

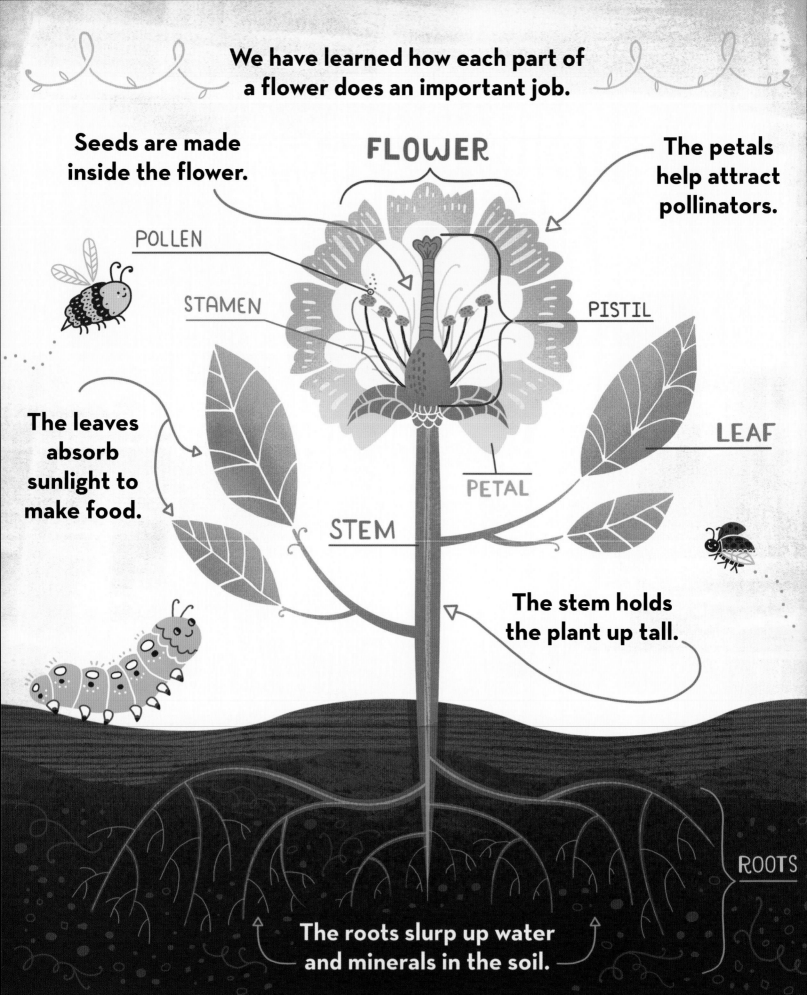

We have learned how each part of
a flower does an important job.

FLOWER

Seeds are made
inside the flower.

The petals
help attract
pollinators.

POLLEN

STAMEN

PISTIL

The leaves
absorb
sunlight to
make food.

LEAF

PETAL

STEM

The stem holds
the plant up tall.

ROOTS

The roots slurp up water
and minerals in the soil.

We also learned that flowers do important things for everyone.

A flower's seeds help spread new plants all over the world.

Plants make fresh air.

OXYGEN

Flowers grow into food for people and animals.

SHADE

Plants also do countless other things!

ANIMAL HABITATS

BEAUTY

What will you plant in your garden?
What will you grow?

Yummy tomatoes?

Sweet-smelling lavender?

Giant sunflowers?

Whatever you
plant in your garden
will be lovely.

Because you know
what's inside a flower
and you understand
the science that
makes flowers special.

Happy flowers
mean a happy earth
for you and me.

SOURCES

I love doing research for my books! Here are some of the books, websites, and places I visited to make this book.

For an expanded list of sources and other educational resources, please visit rachelignotofsky.com and follow me on Instagram at @rachelignotofsky

BOOKS

Karr, Susan, Jeneen Interlandi, and Anne Houtman. *Scientific American Environmental Science for a Changing World*. New York: W. H. Freeman and Company, 2018.

Niehaus, Theodore F. *A Field Guide to Pacific States Wildflowers: Washington, Oregon, California, and Adjacent Areas*. Peterson Field Guides. New York: Houghton Mifflin Harcourt, 1998.

Rao, DK, and JJ Kaur. *New Living Science Biology for Class 9*. Delhi: Ratna Sagar, 2006.

WEBSITES

US Forest Service
fs.usda.gov

Wildflower Search
wildflowersearch.org

Santa Monica Mountains Trails Council
smmtc.org

PLACES I VISITED

The Huntington Library, Art Museum, and Botanical Gardens

Eaton Canyon Natural Area and Nature Center

Big Basin Redwoods State Park

RESOURCES FOR READERS

Want to learn more about plants and flowers? Here are some of my favorite websites and books!

WEBSITES

DK Find Out! Plants
dkfindout.com/us/animals-and-nature/plants

Kids Gardening
kidsgardening.org/garden-activities/

National Park Service
nps.gov/index.htm

BOOKS

Aston, Dianna Hutts. *A Seed Is Sleepy*. San Francisco: Chronicle, 2007.

Ehlert, Lois. *Planting a Rainbow*. New York: Houghton Mifflin Harcourt, 2013.

Gibbons, Gail. *Flowers*. New York: Holiday House, 2020.

Jordan, Helene J., and Loretta Krupinski. *How a Seed Grows*. New York: HarperCollins, 2015.

Willis, Kathy, and Katie Scott. *Botanicum: Welcome to the Museum*. Boston: Big Picture Press, 2017.

Zommer, Yuval, Elisa Biondi, Scott Taylor, and Barbara Taylor. *The Big Book of Blooms*. New York: Thames & Hudson, 2020.